D1415671

THE STORY OF THE
LOS ANGELES
LAKERS

CREATIVE EDUCATION

Published by Creative Education
123 South Broad Street
Mankato, Minnesota 56001
Creative Education is an imprint of The Creative Company.

DESIGN AND PRODUCTION BY **EVANSDAY DESIGN**

PHOTOGRAPHS BY Associated Press, AP, Getty Images (Andrew D.
Bernstein / NBAE, Ken Biggs / Stone, Lisa Blumenfeld, Nathaniel S.
Butler / NBAE, Gary Dineen / NBAE, Stephen Dunn, NBAE Photos
/ NBAE, Mike Powell, Wen Roberts / NBAE), SportsChrome
(Brian Spurlock)

LIBRARY OF CONGRESS CATALOGING-IN-PUBLICATION DATA

LeBoutillier, Nate.
The story of the Los Angeles Lakers / by Nate LeBoutillier.
p. cm. — (The NBA—a history of hoops)
Includes index.
ISBN-13: 978-1-58341-411-8
1. Los Angeles Lakers (Basketball team)—History—
Juvenile literature. I. Title. II. Series.

GV885.52.L67L43 2006
796.323'64'0979494   2005051405

First edition

9 8 7 6 5 4 3 2 1

COVER PHOTO: *Kobe Bryant*

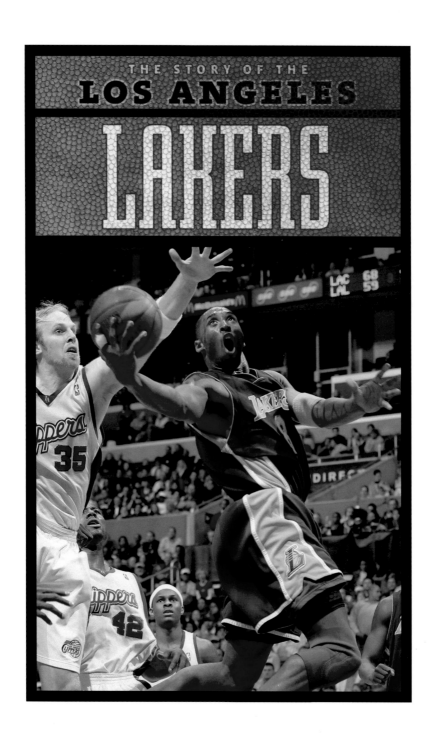

THE STORY OF THE
LOS ANGELES
LAKERS

NATE LeBOUTILLIER

CREATIVE ◖ EDUCATION

A shot clangs

OFF THE RIM. IN A DAZZLING UNIFORM OF PURPLE AND GOLD, TALL CENTER KAREEM ABDUL-JABBAR STRETCHES TO SNATCH THE BOUNDING BASKETBALL, WHIRLS, AND FIRES A ONE-ARMED BASEBALL PASS TO GUARD BYRON SCOTT AT HALF-COURT. SCOTT SHOVELS THE BALL TO POINT GUARD MAGIC JOHNSON, WHO'S STREAKING ACROSS THE MIDDLE OF THE FLOOR LIKE A METEOR ON FIRE. MAGIC BARELY TOUCHES THE BALL, IT SEEMS, BEFORE FLIPPING A NO-LOOK, BEHIND-THE-BACK PASS TO FORWARD JAMES WORTHY. WHEN WORTHY DUNKS THE BALL THROUGH THE RIM, IT'S JUST ANOTHER TWO POINTS FOR THE LAKERS' "SHOWTIME" FAST BREAK.

U.S.C ↗

LOS ANGELES LAKERS
Los Angeles California

LAKER BEGINNINGS

1

LOS ANGELES, CALIFORNIA, IS A CITY KNOWN FOR ITS sprawling size. The city and its surrounding communities are spread over an area nearly 50 miles wide. Los Angeles's warm climate and beautiful setting between the San Gabriel mountains to the east and the Pacific Ocean to the west have lured people to the "City of Angels" for more than 200 years.

Home to Hollywood's movie and television industries, Los Angeles added another form of entertainment when a National Basketball Association (NBA) team called the Minneapolis Lakers moved to southern California in 1960. The Lakers started out in Minnesota in 1947 as a member of the National Basketball League (NBL), and their first big star was a 6-foot-10 and 245-pound giant named George Mikan.

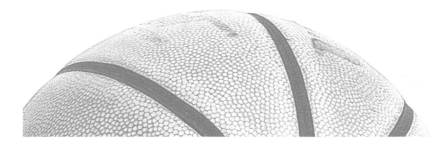

Early Lakers great George Mikan is still remembered as one of the most dominant centers of all time

LAKERS

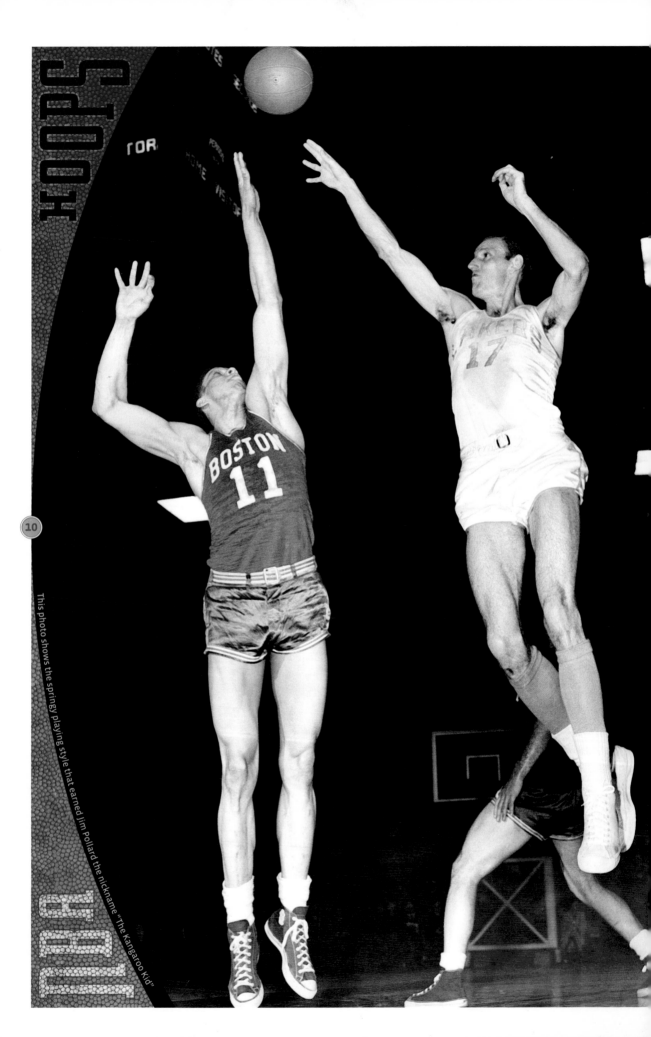

NBA

This photo shows the springy playing style that earned Jim Pollard the nickname "The Kangaroo Kid"

Although he looked studious in his wire-rim glasses, Mikan was a terror on the court, tossing up soft hook shots with either hand on offense and repeatedly blocking opponents' shots on defense. With Mikan, the Minneapolis Lakers easily won the 1948 league championship. "George was the game's first great big man," said Boston Celtics coaching legend Red Auerbach. "He was so big and strong, and yet he moved like a cat."

The next year, Minneapolis jumped to a rival league, the Basketball Association of America (BAA), and the Lakers powered their way to a second consecutive championship. In 1949, the NBL and the BAA merged to form the NBA, and the Lakers became the new league's elite team. In the NBA's first playoffs, the Lakers swaggered through the early rounds, then topped the Syracuse Nationals in the Finals to claim the very first NBA championship.

Mikan—aided by forward Jim "The Kangaroo Kid" Pollard, guard Slater Martin, and forward-center Vern Mikkelsen—pushed the Lakers to three more NBA titles in the next four years, but before the 1954–55 season, Mikan retired. By the end of the 1957–58 season, the Lakers had sunk to last place, and their popularity in Minnesota waned. Not even the addition of high-flying guard Elgin Baylor in 1958 sparked fan interest. By 1960, the Lakers were looking for a new home.

JERRY "THE LOGO" WEST

It is stitched into every jersey and every pair of shorts worn in the NBA. It adorns headbands, socks, and wristbands. It appears on courts and basketball backboards. *It* is the NBA logo, a red, white, and blue image that has become the symbol of the NBA. But who is the man in the silhouette? Why, it's Jerry West, Hall of Fame guard for the Los Angeles Lakers. The silhouette of West was chosen because he was one of the classiest ballplayers the league had ever known, and one of the most successful. At 6-foot-2 and 185 pounds, West was neither big nor terribly athletic. But a strong will to win made the image of "Mr. Clutch" one that the NBA has taken pride in brandishing through the years.

13

LAKERS

Sometimes called "the man with a thousand moves," explosive scorer Elgin Baylor was an 11-time All-Star

THE LAKERS HEAD WEST

BEFORE THE 1960–61 SEASON, THE LAKERS MOVED to Los Angeles and drafted guard Jerry West from the University of West Virginia. West and Baylor quickly became one of the league's deadliest back-court duos, and the Lakers began to dominate the NBA's Western Division.

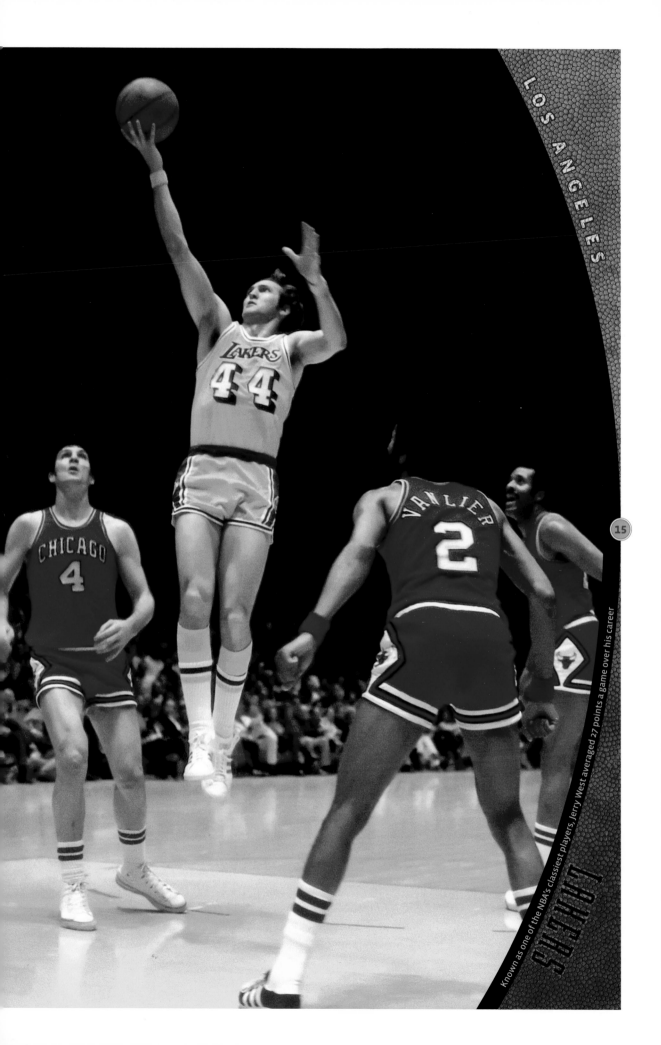

15

LAKERS

Known as one of the NBA's classiest players, Jerry West averaged 27 points a game over his career

Wilt Chamberlain seemed impossibly long when he soared to drop the ball in the basket or grab a rebound

Five times in the years between 1962 and 1968, the Lakers captured the Western Division crown and squared off against the Eastern Division champion Boston Celtics in the NBA Finals, but the Celtics went home with the title every time. In 1968, Los Angeles traded for center Wilt Chamberlain, the most feared player in the league. The Lakers made the Finals in both 1969 and 1970 but lost in seven games both years.

The 1971–72 season finally brought an end to the Lakers' frustration. Although Baylor was forced to retire early that season due to a knee injury, forward Harold "Happy" Hairston and guards Gail Goodrich and Pat Riley stepped up to carry the load. The determined Lakers won 69 regular-season games, including an NBA-record 33 in a row. Chamberlain concentrated on rebounding and defense and let his teammates do much of the scoring. This team effort led to another trip to the NBA Finals. This time Los Angeles broke through, beating the New York Knicks in five games. "This city's been waiting a long time," said Chamberlain. "It's a great feeling to be a champion."

HISTORIC HOT STREAK

Sometimes a team gets hot—so hot that nothing seems to go wrong. For more than two months, from November 5, 1971, to January 9, 1972, the Lakers won 33 games in a row—a record for consecutive victories in professional team sports. But the magic had to end sometime, and it did when the Milwaukee Bucks' 7-foot-2 center Kareem Abdul-Jabbar came up big in Milwaukee, outplaying the Lakers' 7-foot-1 Wilt Chamberlain. The defending NBA champion Bucks won 120–104, with the 24-year-old Abdul-Jabbar outscoring the 35-year-old Chamberlain 39–15. "I'm sorry the streak is over," said Lakers guard Jerry West. "I wanted it to go on forever." The Lakers found consolation in winning the NBA title that season, and—some four years later—in signing the man who helped break their streak, Abdul-Jabbar.

MAGIC USHERS IN "SHOWTIME"

3

AFTER A FEW MORE SEASONS, BOTH CHAMBERLAIN and West retired. Without their stars, the Lakers were still a good team, but not a great one. Then, before the 1975–76 season, the Lakers made a blockbuster trade for another outstanding big man, getting center Kareem Abdul-Jabbar from the Milwaukee Bucks.

The first player to log 20 NBA seasons, center Kareem Abdul-Jabbar could score even when triple-teamed

Magic Johnson was huge for a guard, which helped him see over opponents and fire long passes

The Lakers built around their big man, acquiring high-scoring forward Jamaal "Silk" Wilkes and point guard Norm Nixon. However, the final piece to the Lakers' championship puzzle came in the 1979 NBA Draft, when Los Angeles chose 6-foot-9 guard Earvin "Magic" Johnson with the first overall pick. Magic was tall and strong enough to play forward or center, but he was also a brilliant passer, ball handler, and leader. With Johnson running the point, the Lakers played a dazzling, fast-breaking style that came to be known as "Showtime."

After the 1979–80 season, the Lakers roared into the NBA Finals, where they met the Philadelphia 76ers and their superstar, Julius "Dr. J" Erving. Los Angeles took a three-games-to-two lead in the series, but Abdul-Jabbar suffered a sprained left ankle and was forced to sit out Game 6. Twenty-year-old Magic then led Los Angeles to victory, scoring 42 points, snaring 15 rebounds, and passing for 7 assists while playing all five positions on the court, including Abdul-Jabbar's center spot. After the win, Magic, the Finals Most Valuable Player (MVP), didn't forget Abdul-Jabbar. "I know your ankle hurts, Kareem," Magic joked, "but why don't you get up and dance, anyway?"

THE HOOK SHOT

It seemed more a ballet move than a basketball shot. The pirouette of the feet, the graceful sweeping of the arm, the arc of the ball—this was the hook shot. Used by many players in the early days of the game, the hook was a sure-fire way to send the ball on its way to the basket without getting it blocked by an opponent, but it took skill and a feathery touch to master. One player above all others, longtime Lakers great Kareem Abdul-Jabbar, made the shot famous. "The first time I shot the hook, I was in fourth grade...," said Abdul-Jabbar, who called his version the "sky hook." "I felt totally at ease with the shot. I was completely confident it would go in, and I've been shooting it ever since."

LOS ANGELES RETURNED TO THE NBA FINALS IN 1982, again versus the 76ers. Led by new coach Pat Riley—a key member of the Lakers' 1972 championship team—the Lakers beat Philadelphia in six games again to claim the franchise's eighth NBA championship. Behind the success was a lot of hard work, as Riley pushed his players to the limit in practice. "He works us like dogs," said Magic Johnson, "but the finished product is so pretty."

Los Angeles added graceful forward James Worthy in 1982 and athletic guard Byron Scott in 1983. In 1985, the Lakers met their old nemesis, the Celtics, in the NBA Finals. The Lakers were crushed 148–114 in Game 1, but they battled back and defeated the Celtics in six games. The championship victory was the Lakers' first Finals win in nine tries against the Celtics. "It is very sweet," said Riley. "Lakers fans have been waiting for this one a long time."

23

Fleet-footed forward James Worthy often finished the Lakers' "Showtime" fast breaks with a dunk

24

Quick and crafty center Vlade Divac led the team in rebounds for four straight seasons in the early '90s

The Lakers went on to win two more NBA championships in the '80s, beating the Celtics again in 1987 and topping the Detroit Pistons in 1988. Their decade-long run of excellence—and Magic's rivalry with Celtics star Larry Bird—helped take the popularity of pro basketball to new heights.

After the 1988–89 season, Abdul-Jabbar retired. The next year, Riley stepped down as head coach. Johnson and Worthy continued on and, with the help of Scott and new center Vlade Divac, led the Lakers to another NBA Finals appearance in 1991. However, the team of the '80s there faced what would be the team of the '90s: the Chicago Bulls. The Lakers won Game 1, but the Bulls and their star, Michael Jordan, captured the next four games and the title.

Early in the 1991–92 season, Johnson shocked the basketball world. The three-time NBA MVP had tested positive for the HIV virus, he said, and was retiring immediately. At the end of the 1993–94 season, the Lakers missed the playoffs for the first time in 18 years.

MAGIC'S RETURN

In a startling November 7, 1991, press conference, legendary guard Magic Johnson admitted that he was infected with HIV, the virus that causes AIDS, and would be forced to retire from the game of basketball. The announcement sent shockwaves through legions of basketball fans everywhere and marked the end of a long Lakers success streak. Magic would make several short-lived comebacks, most dramatically in the 1992 NBA All-Star Game in which he scored 25 points, had 9 assists, and won the game's MVP honors. "It's like I'm in a dream right now, and I don't ever want to wake up," said Johnson, who was voted into the game by fans. "Because for one day, I got the NBA back in me. This was like the perfect ending to the story."

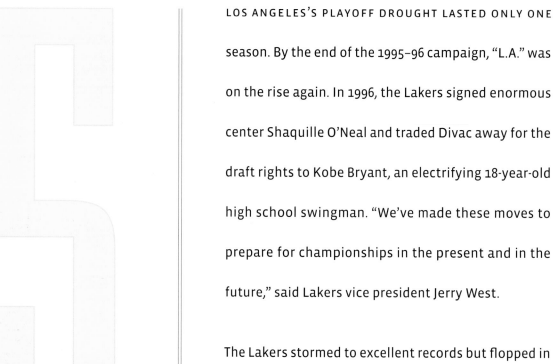

SHAQ, KOBE, AND PHIL

LOS ANGELES'S PLAYOFF DROUGHT LASTED ONLY ONE season. By the end of the 1995–96 campaign, "L.A." was on the rise again. In 1996, the Lakers signed enormous center Shaquille O'Neal and traded Divac away for the draft rights to Kobe Bryant, an electrifying 18-year-old high school swingman. "We've made these moves to prepare for championships in the present and in the future," said Lakers vice president Jerry West.

The Lakers stormed to excellent records but flopped in the playoffs three straight seasons. In 1999, Phil Jackson, who had won six titles as coach of the Bulls, came out of retirement to coach the Lakers. Jackson immediately put his stamp on the team, installing the complicated triangle offense that the Bulls had used. The Lakers posted a 67–15 mark and marched to the 2000 NBA Finals, where they faced the Indiana Pacers. Behind O'Neal's 41 points in Game 6, Los Angeles captured its 12th NBA title. "This is why I came here," proclaimed O'Neal. "I wanted to be a champion."

LAKERS

Weighing well over 300 pounds, Shaquille O'Neal reigned as the NBA's largest and most powerful player

NBA

1270 AM KESS
PRIMERA EM
NOTICIAS Y DEPORTES

Kobe Bryant's spectacular moves and sky-high leaping ability made him the Lakers' feature attraction

O'Neal and his teammates were champions the next two seasons as well. The Lakers "three-peated" by defeating the New Jersey Nets in 2001 and the Philadelphia 76ers in 2002 and looked to be on the verge of a dynasty. But all was not well in Lakerland. The two biggest stars on the team, Shaq and Kobe, bickered off and on the court, struggling to share the spotlight. The Lakers brought in two future Hall-of-Famers—forward Karl Malone and point guard Gary Payton—in 2003 and reached the Finals in 2004, but the overconfident team was then embarrassed by the Detroit Pistons, losing four games in a row.

Following the disappointing loss, the Lakers were dismantled. O'Neal was traded to Miami, Payton was traded to Boston, Karl Malone retired, and Phil Jackson left basketball for a year before returning as coach. In 2004–05, what was left of the Lakers went 33–49 and missed the playoffs for the first time in 10 years. The Lakers planned their rebuilding process around Bryant, do-it-all forward Lamar Odom, and their top pick in the 2005 NBA Draft, Andrew Bynum, a 7-foot and 295-pound 17-year-old with a keen resemblance to O'Neal.

Historically, the Lakers have been one of the NBA's greatest and most glamorous franchises, from the days of George Mikan to the Showtime of the '80s to the dominating tandem of Shaquille O'Neal and Kobe Bryant. Lakers fans have come to expect nothing but the best, and the rest of the NBA can count on the Lakers vying for another title soon.

LAKERS BIG MEN

Being tall can have its advantages, especially in professional basketball. The Lakers have been especially blessed with big men, outfitting four of the best centers ever to play the game in the gold and purple. These giants each put together stellar careers, and the numbers are impressive. George Mikan stood 6-foot-10 and led the Lakers to four championships in eight seasons (1948–56); 7-foot-1 Wilt Chamberlain played five seasons for the Lakers (1968–73), winning one championship; 7-foot-2 Kareem Abdul-Jabbar played 14 seasons for the Lakers (1975–89) and won five championships; and 7-foot-1 Shaquille O'Neal played eight seasons for the Lakers (1996–2004), winning three championships. That's more than 28 feet of center in 35 seasons for 13 Lakers championships. The Lakers' top 2005 draft pick was 7-foot (and growing) teenaged center Andrew Bynum.

31

Forward Lamar Odom was a rare combination of talent, leading the 2005–06 Lakers in both assists and rebounds

INDEX